BRITISH GEOLOGICAL SURVEY
Natural Environment Research Council

CU00592029

Geology of the country around Bangor

Explanation for 1:50 000 geological sheet 106 (England & Wales)

M. F. Howells, A. J. Reedman and B. E. Leveridge

1835 Geological Survey of Great Britain

150 Years of Service to the Nation

1985 British Geological Survey

Bibliographical reference

**Howells, M. F., Reedman, A. J., and
Leveridge, B. E.** 1985. Geology of the country
around Bangor. *Explan. 1:50 000 sheet, Br. Geol.
Surv.*, Sheet 106, England and Wales.

ISBN 0 11 884417 2

London   Her Majesty's Stationery Office   1985

Contents

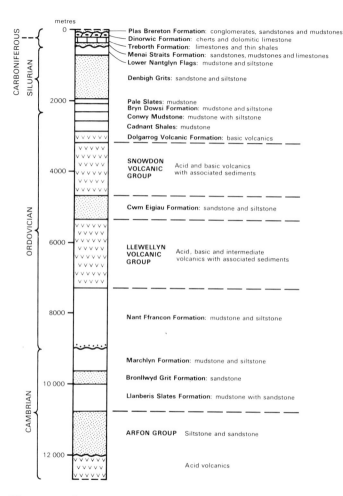

Figure 1 Simplified vertical section.

1   Introduction and geological setting

The area covered by the 1:50 000 Sheet (106) extends between the Conwy Valley in the east, the Menai Straits in the west, the Llanberis Pass in the south and the vicinity of Penmaenmawr in the north. It is renowned for its spectacular mountain scenery—including eleven of the fourteen 3000-ft peaks in the Snowdonia National Park: Elidir Fawr, Y Garn, Glyder Fawr, Glyder Fach, Tryfan, Pen yr Ole Wen, Carnedd Dafydd, Carnedd Llewelyn, Yr Elen, Foel Grach and Foel Fras.

We wrote this brief description of the geology to be read in conjunction with the map. We describe the succession of strata occurring in the area, from the base upwards. Figure 1 is a simplified vertical section, and on the 1:50 000 sheet there are sections that show more detail. For each element of the succession we have nominated a locality which is particularly characteristic and which can be readily found on the 1:50 000 or 1:25 000 sheets: in an area as well exposed as this, there are many other good localities for most of the formations.

Most of the ground is owned privately or by the Forestry Commission. The owners' permission should be obtained for access to any areas away from public footpaths. Furthermore, visitors to localities that are freely open to the public should conform to the Code of Conduct for Geology, published by the Geologists' Association; it is reproduced at the end of this book.

Throughout the district there is evidence of its long occupation by man. The tombs of the earliest immigrants are evident in the gromlechs above Penmaenmawr and west of Roe Wen, which date back to the Bronze Age about 2000 years ago. Hill forts such as Braich y ddinas above Penmaenmawr, now demolished by the local quarry, were possibly occupied before the time of the Romans. The earliest domestic architecture is to be seen in the hut circles, such as in Cwm Dulyn, which may have been occupied from the Bronze Age to well into the Middle Ages. Certain roads shown the influence of the Roman occupation: one such passes through Bwlch y Ddeufaen, and linked Segontium at Caernarfon with Caerhun in the Conwy Valley and Chester.

In more recent times, probably up to the middle of the 19th century, farming life followed a pattern called 'transhumance'. Livestock and people wintered in a lowland farm or *hendre* and moved for the summer to a mountain farm or *hafod*. Witness to the practice in the high valleys to the west of the Conwy Valley are place-names in which hafod is an element. For the most part the agricultural use of the district in modern times is restricted by the hills, soils and climate to sheep and cattle grazing. Forestry is also important; arable farming is mostly confined to the low ground near the coast and along the Afon Conwy Valley.

Most of the upland lakes have been harnessed at some time as a source of water or for generating hydroelectricity. By far the largest such enterprise is the recently completed Dinorwic Pumped Storage Scheme, linking Llyn Peris to the reservoir at Llyn Marchlyn. Industrial development in the district has been dominated by two products, both of geological interest: non-ferrous metalliferous minerals and slate. The most important area for metalliferous mineral extraction was the Llanrwst mining district to the west of the Conwy Valley, which was developed in the mid-19th century for lead and zinc. After 1914 the level of activity declined sharply although one mine was worked intermittently to the late 1950s. The slate industry also expanded most rapidly in the mid-19th century. The vast slate tips of the Dinorwic and Penrhyn Quarries now lie as monuments to this once-important industry. The Penrhyn Quarry is still worked on a much smaller scale.

At the present time the main industry is tourism. Each year an estimated four million people visit the area between April and October. Many of these are attracted to the hills, and it is estimated that some 400 000 reach the summit of Snowdon each year. As it has become easier to reach the area from the large conurbations in England, so it has become an important open-air classroom for field-based studies, which can range in a short distance from intertidal areas in the Menai Straits to the high mountain ridges.

HISTORY OF GEOLOGICAL WORK

The geology of the Bangor area has been studied since the early years of the 19th century. William Smith, the 'father of British geology', apparently visited the area, and designated most of the rocks there as 'Killas and Slate' on his map published in 1815. Adam Sedgwick began work there in 1831 (Clarke and Hughes, 1890) and for part of this time was accompanied by Charles Darwin. Sedgwick's map (1845) on the scale of 1 inch to 8 miles was followed by Daniel Sharpe's map (1846) on the scale of 1 inch to 5½ miles. These maps were the first to show the broad outlines of the structure, and the general boundaries between sedimentary and igneous rocks.

In 1846 the systematic mapping of the area on the scale of 1 inch to 1 mile was begun by the Geological Survey under the guidance of A. C. Ramsay and by 1852 was completed. Eventually Ramsay (1866, 1881) produced two editions of the classic North Wales Memoir, in the second of which the first comprehensive account of the geology appeared. A little later, Harker (1889) made a further distinctive contribution with a description of the volcanic rocks in his essay on the Bala Volcanic Series.

Work in the early years of this century was dominated by Greenly, whose main effort was concentrated on the mapping of Anglesey. This work formed the basis of a one-inch geological map of Anglesey (the Anglesey Special Sheet) and an accompanying memoir published by the Geological Survey (1919). Subsequently Greenly extended his work into the Bangor area of the mainland (1944, 1945, 1946).

It was, however, the Williams brothers, Howel and David, who made the major contribution to geological knowledge of the district. Howel Williams (1922) published a paper on the igneous rocks of the Capel Curig district, prior to his classic map and paper on the geology of Snowdon (1927) as far north as the Llanberis Pass. David Williams (1930) extended the mapping of the stratigraphic sequence established by his brother into the area between Nant Ffrancon and Nant Peris. Later Davies (1936) described the sequence of Ordovician rocks in the Trefriw district and postulated correlations with the sequence in Central Snowdonia.

Much of this work was concerned with the stratigraphy and petrography of the succession. One conclusion drawn by all the early workers was that because the sedimentary rocks contained marine fossils, they must therefore have been deposited in the sea. Accordingly, it was reasonable to conclude that the extrusive volcanic rocks within the sequence were also emplaced under water.

In the 1950s there was a resurgence of interest in the area following the recognition by Oliver (1954) and subsequent confirmation by Rast, Beavon and Fitch (1958), that many of the acidic volcanic rocks that previously were regarded as rhyolites were in fact ash-flow tuffs or ignimbrites. The recognition of ash-flow volcanism is relatively recent, the process only being comprehensively defined in the early 1960s. This advance resolved problems which had exercised volcanologists for many years (for a resumé see Chapin and Elston, 1979) concerning rocks that seemingly had both pyroclastic and magmatic characters. The first clear observations were made by Anderson and Flett (1903) and Lacroix (1903, 1904) on the 1902 eruption of Montagne Pelée on Martinique and Soufrière on St Vincent in the West Indies. At St Pierre on Martinique about 30 000 people were killed by the blast of hot gas that accompanied the eruption of May 1902. Lacroix termed this type of eruption a *'nuée ardente'* (glowing cloud), made up of 'an emulsion of solid materials in a mixture of water vapour and gas at high temperature'. Marshall (1935), working on the volcanic rocks of North Island, New Zealand, coined the term ignimbrite to describe the rocks formed from a *nuée ardente* as defined by Lacroix. However, although successive workers, including Howel Williams, continued to describe the varying characters of the products of these eruptions, it was not until the papers by R. L. Smith (1960a, 1960b) and Ross and Smith (1961) that the model of ash-flow volcanism was firmly established.

Ash-flows comprise disintegrated fragments of vesiculated magmatic glass, shards, and crystals that are violently erupted together with vitric dust and suspended in a hot gas-charged cloud. The flows move downslope, often at great speed and for long distances, and as the momentum lessens, clastic particles settle from the basal layers of the flow. The resulting deposit, an ash-flow tuff, may locally be hot enough on emplacement for the glass fragments to fuse together and be flattened under the weight of accumulated material on top. A tuff in this condition is described as welded. The only characteristic in ancient rocks to indicate that they have been welded is the flattening of shards and pumice. It was this fabric that was recognised by Oliver (1954), and Rast, Beavon and Fitch (1958), in some of the acidic rocks of the Bangor district. However, because the earlier researchers on ash-flow tuffs had considered that they could only be deposited on land, the palaeogeographical setting of the Ordovician volcanism in North Wales was hastily revised to provide for widespread periodic emergence of land upon which to emplace the extensive ash-flows.

Our recent surveys, which have led to the publication of the 1:50 000 map, were conducted against this background. They have now shown that an ash-flow can transgress from land into water and still retain sufficient heat on emplacement for the fabric to weld (Francis and Howells, 1973; Howells and Leveridge, 1980). With this model it is unnecessary to propose that the sea-floor must be uplifted prior to the eruption and emplacement of each ash-flow tuff.

REGIONAL TECTONIC SETTING

The Bangor district is mostly composed of rocks of Palaeozoic age; within the district it is possible to identify many of the major components in the evolution of Wales during the Palaeozoic era. In early Palaeozoic times, Wales was the site of a marine basin in which sedimentary rocks accumulated, partly in deep water and partly on shallow shelves. There was intermittent volcanism at various centres across the basin. It was bounded to the north-west by an Irish Sea landmass (Jones, 1938; Jackson, 1961), which separated it from the Leinster-Lake District Basin still further to the north-west. Both these basins were situated close to a convergent plate boundary between the oceanic plate of the Iapetus Ocean (Wilson, 1966; Harland and Gayer 1972) to the north-west and a continental plate to the south-east. The Welsh Basin was undoubtedly ensialic, that is it was sited on continental rather than oceanic crust.

The Iapetus Ocean closed gradually throughout the early Palaeozoic. The oceanic plate was subducted beneath the bounding continental plates, and this subduction gave rise to volcanism at the continental margins, resulting in the emplacement of intrusive and extrusive volcanic rocks in the marginal basins. With the complete closure of the ocean and the final collision of its bounding continental plates during late Silurian to early Devonian times, the strata were deformed and uplifted into the mountain chain referred to as the Caledonides.

From the Cambrian and Ordovician rocks of the district it is possible to interpret the evolution of the Lower Palaeozoic basin, and local variations in its form, by the changing characters of the accumulated sedimentary rocks and by the recognition of volcanic centres and the disposition of the extrusive volcanic rocks. The influence of contemporaneous tectonism on both sedimentation and volcanism can also be recognised. The later stages in the development of the basin can be interpreted from the Silurian rocks which outcrop to the east of the Conwy Valley.

Following the closure of the Iapetus Ocean and the upheaval and erosion of the Caledonian mountain chain, the seas of the early Carboniferous period began to encroach on the area. Around the edge of North Wales Carboniferous sediments, mostly carbonate and shell-rich, lie with profound unconformity on Lower Palaeozoic rocks (Figure 1).

In the Bangor district there is no indication whether Mesozoic rocks once extended into the area. The next interpretable geological event after the Carboniferous is represented by a few thin Tertiary dykes which intersect the Lower Palaeozoic rocks. The final geological episode that profoundly affected the area was the Quaternary glaciation, of which there is much evidence, both erosional and depositional, in the spectacular scenery of Snowdonia.

ARFON GROUP

The Arfon Group lies at the base of the sequence. It comprises the Padarn Tuff Formation together with the Minffordd, Bangor and Fachwen formations, not separately shown on Figure 1, and is broadly equivalent to the Arvonian Series of Greenly (1945). This he regarded as possibly of Precambrian age although current opinion (Reedman and others, 1984) favours an early Cambrian age.

The Arfon Group was deposited during a period of extensional tectonism in which the basement to the group was fragmented by normal faulting. Small, rapidly subsiding, fault-bounded structural and topographic depressions were formed, interspersed with uptilted blocks. The extrusion of acid and, to a lesser extent, basic volcanics accompanied the tectonism. Rapid lateral and vertical variation in the facies of the Arfon Group sediments reflect continued active faulting and changes in the disposition of minor basins and blocks (Reedman and others, 1984). At the top of the group there is evidence of a more general subsidence and the establishment of a broader marine basin deepening towards the south-east.

Padarn Tuff Formation (PdT)[1] The Padarn Tuff Formation is partly uncovered in two ridges, near Bangor and Llyn Padarn (Figure 2) and comprises acidic ash-flow tuffs. Typically these are strongly welded, and contain conspicuous crystals of bipyramidal quartz and albite feldspar. Locally there are thin beds of possible air-fall tuff and rhyolite lava, but both ridges are dominated by welded ash-flow tuffs with little evidence of the bounding surfaces of individual flows. Study of the orientation of welding fabrics in the Llyn Padarn area suggests that the tuffs are at least 800 m thick, and a gravity survey indicates that locally the tuffs are 2000 m thick.

The Bangor and Padarn ridges are aligned along a NE−SW Caledonoid trend, and the great thickness and uniformity of lithology imply that the tuffs were entrapped within a volcano-tectonic depression (Reedman and others, 1984).
Locality:[2] *Old road cutting, south west side of Llyn Padarn* [560 622].

Figure 2 View into Llanberis Pass from south-east of Llanberis. Padarn Tuff Formation in foreground, Ordovician volcanic and sedimentary rocks in the distant high ridges. (L2233)

---

1 PdT: this, and similar symbols given later, relate to symbols used on the 1:50 000 sheet.
2 Localities shown thus are selected to illustrate the typical features of the unit described.

Minffordd Formation (Mdd) Faulting continued after the deposition of the Padarn Tuff Formation, accompanied by differential erosion, subsidence and sporadic volcanic activity. In the Bangor area the Padarn Tuff Formation is overlain by the Minffordd Formation which was deposited in a rapidly subsiding depression to the east of the Aber-Dinlle Fault. The depression extends to the west into Anglesey, where the formation is represented by the Baron Hill Beds of Greenly (1919).

The Minffordd Formation is a sequence at least 1500 m thick of laminated siltstones, acidic air-fall tuffs and tuffites intercalated with volcanogenic conglomerates, sandstones and thin ash-flow tuffs. The sandstones and conglomerates are lithic greywackes and arkoses probably representing mass-flows from a shoreline environment into deeper water. They contain variable proportions of acid and basic lithic clasts, the former derived mainly from the Padarn Tuff and the latter either from the extrusive basalts which form a part of the Gwna Group in Anglesey or from basalts extruded onto the Padarn Tuff to the south of the Bangor area.
Localities: Along track from Pant-caerhun [573 694] towards Tai'r-ffynnon [566 698[. Roadcuts on Bangor Bypass [568 694].

Bangor Formation (Bno) The Minffordd Formation was faulted, tilted to the east and locally eroded prior to the unconformable deposition of the Bangor Formation. This formation is some 240 m thick on Bangor Mountain. It consists of sandstone and conglomerate composed predominantly of clasts of Padarn Tuff, together with sandstone, mica-schist and granite clasts, overlain by laminated siltstone, tuffite and tuff with some intercalated sandstone. In places the laminated sequence is slump-folded and the sandstones are turbiditic, reflecting contemporaneous instability of the shelf area.
Locality: Bangor [585 722].

Fachwen Formation (Fa) To the east of the Aber-Dinlle Fault the Fachwen Formation rests either unconformably or disconformably on the Padarn Tuff Formation. It thickens westwards from 40 m near Dinorwic to over 500 m on the west side of the Padarn ridge. The basal beds, which are conglomerates and sandstones, lie on intensely welded ash-flow tuff, and are themselves locally interbedded with thin acidic ash-flow and air-fall tuffs, indicating that volcanism recurred sporadically in the vicinity. The conglomerates, consisting mainly of sub-angular clasts of welded tuff, and the sandstones, with distinctive quartz crystals derived from the underlying tuff, probably represent rapidly accumulating alluvial fans of material derived largely from local fault-scarps, and fluvial deposits. Well-rounded clasts of quartzite, mica schist, granite and jasper came from further away. Higher in the sequence there are siltstones and sandstones, locally with conglomerates and tuffites, and there is some indication towards the top of the formation of a more general subsidence which led to the establishment of the broad marine basin in which the overlying sediments were deposited.

The precise correlation between the Fachwen Formation, to the east of the Aber-Dinlle Fault, and the Minffordd and Bangor formations to the west, has not yet been established, but the Fachwen Formation is probably the lateral equivalent of parts of both formations.
Localities: Fachwen [574 618], footpaths between Bigil [579 623] and Deiniolen [579 633].

Llanberis Slates Formation (LlbS) The Llanberis Slates Formation is renowned as the source of the slates that have been worked in the Llanberis and Bethesda area, and led to the growth of both communities. The distribution of the formation at outcrop is clearly marked by numerous small quarries and trial pits that were excavated beyond the main quarrying complexes at Dinorwic and Penrhyn (Figure 3, overleaf).

The formation mainly comprises purple and blue-grey silty mudstones, that accumulated in a broad marine basin which deepened to the south-east. Intermittent instability in the source area to the north-west caused turbidity flows which produced incursions of coarse sand. Most distinctively, these turbidites include rip-up clasts of silty mudstone and, in places, fill chanels eroded in the underlying muds. They were probably deposited as submarine fans, and their more distal facies are thin bands of graded siltstone and fine sandstone intercalated in the slate sequence.

Bedding in the purple siltstones is locally well developed, common-   **5**

Figure 3 Penrhyn Slate Quarry, Bethesda; northern Carneddau ridge in far distance. Excavations in cleaved silty mudstones of the Llanberis States Formation. (L1450)

ly accentuated by sharply contrasting green bands as a result of the reduction of iron in individual beds. Similar reduction produced the characteristic green spotting. On fresh surfaces of large slabs of cut slate disturbed bedding can be distinguished; this ranges from slumped continuous beds of silty mudstone and muddy siltstone to totally disintegrated bedding. These beds probably produce the most perfect slates because they contain no well-defined bedding planes or lithological contacts to interrupt the cleavage.

Trilobites found near the top of the formation include *Pseudatops viola* and other forms (Wood, 1969; Howell and Stubblefield, 1950). Bassett and others (1976, p.641) correlated this fauna with the top of the Olenellid Zone in the middle of the Comley Series (Lower Cambrian).

Localities: Penrhyn Slate Quarry, Bethesda [620 650], *Quarry Nature Trail at Padarn Country Park* [586 603].

Bronllwyd Grit Formation (BGr) Typically the formation is dominated by thick beds of coarse-grained green-grey massive sandstone with minor mudstone partings which are commonly manganiferous. The base is sharply defined by coarse conglomeratic sandstone overlying and locally cutting down into silty mudstones. The sandstones show graded and cross-bedding, and represent turbiditic incursions of shallow-water sands into a depositional environment of deep-water mud. Such incursions indicate repeated tectonic activity and uplift in the source area to the north-west. In the north of the area the intercalated mudstones are better developed.

Because the sandstones are resistant to erosion the formation forms a prominent feature along much of its outcrop. Towards the top the sandstone component decreases, the individual beds are thinner, and the formation grades up into the Marchlyn Formation. The age of the Bronllwyd Grit is uncertain but the erosive base and gradational top favour its being part of the Upper Cambrian sequence.

Localities: Roadside exposures towards south-east end of Llyn Peris [595 590], *Clogwyn Mawr* [592 585].

Marchlyn Formation (MaF) At its base the Marchlyn Formation is dark grey mudstone with fine sandstone laminae and in places impersistent beds of coarser sandstone and ironstone. Above, it is typically made up of pale grey siltstones containing thin flaggy ripple-marked sandstone beds with convoluted internal bedding laminations. Near its top the formation includes the Carnedd y Filiast Grit member (Figure 4), which locally is overlain by grey siltstones. The Carnedd y Filiast Grit (CGr) is a medium- to coarse-grained, massive to even bedded, quartzose and locally pebbly sandstone, with graded and cross-bedding and locally ripple-marked bedding planes. It contains the inarticulate brachiopod *Lingulella davisii*, the trilobite *Olenus*? and abundant trace fossils including *Cruziana semiplicata*. These can be referred to the earlier parts of the Upper Cambrian Merioneth Series (Crimes, 1970).

The sedimentary character of the Marchlyn Formation indicates a change from the active basinal deposition of the underlying sequence to progessively more stable, shallower-water conditions. The well-sorted character of the Carnedd y Filiast Grit suggests reworking of previously deposited sediments prior to temporary emergence, tilting and erosion at the end of the Cambrian period (see below).
Localities: Marchlyn Formation, Marchlyn Mawr [615 619], Carnedd y Filiast Grit, Cwm Graianog [622 626].

Figure 4 Cwm Graianog. Ordovician 'Graianog Sandstone' lying with slight angular unconformity on Cambrian, Carnedd y Filiast Grit. Mynydd Perfedd Granite intrusion at left of photograph. (L2662)

The basal Ordovician sediments were deposited during a marine transgression over tilted eroded fault blocks of Cambrian strata. Rocks of Arenig age overstep the Merioneth Series and there is no evidence in the area for the Tremadoc Series. The unconformity increases in magnitude to the west, indicating that uplift was greatest in that direction (Greenly, 1944). East of Bethesda and Llanberis, pre-Arenig tilting and erosion was slight (Reedman and others, 1983) but, near Bangor, Arenig rocks lie with angular unconformity on early Cambrian tuffs and sediments.

Nant Ffrancon Formation (NFr) Along much of its outcrop the base of the Nant Ffrancon Formation and of the Ordovician (Howells and others, 1983) is taken at the base of the Graianog Sandstone (Gra) of Arenig age (Reedman and others, 1983) although locally no distinct sandstone member is present. The sandstone is typically medium- to fine-grained, poorly bedded, argillaceous and bioturbated; the oncolitic phosphate concretion *Bolopora undosa* is common. In Cwm Graianog [624 624] the sandstone lies with slight angular unconformity on the Carnedd y Filiast Grit (Figure 4), and pebbles of the grit occur towards the base. In the Bangor area the basal sandstone is locally well sorted and quartzose, and lies with marked unconformity on the Arfon Group. The overlying bioturbated sandstone contains an impersistent bed of pisolitic ironstone. Trace fossils present include *Phycodes circinatum* and *Teichichnus* sp.

The Graianog Sandstone grades up into dark grey silty mudstone which is the predominant lithology of the Nant Ffrancon Formation (Figure 5, overleaf). Locally the mudstones contain phosphatic nodules; elsewhere they are pyritic. Sedimentary ironstone of early Llanvirn age has been mined at a number of localities low in the formation (Llandegai (590 696), Aber (670 724)), and towards the top there is at least one further impersistent bed of pisolitic ironstone. The highest mudstones of the formation are darker, although they have bleached weathered surfaces. Upward through the formation the rocks reflect a deepening of the depositional environment, although there were temporary periods of shallow deposition when the pisolitic ironstone beds were formed.

Locally, as on the south-west flank of Carnedd Llewelyn, the uppermost mudstones show small-scale slumped bedding and contain lenses of mudflow breccia. These breccias were produced by seismic activity that caused the accumulated sediments, which were in various stages of lithification, to be unstable and to move down the slope. Contained in the breccias are clasts of hornfelsed mudstone and felsite, indicative of the unroofing of high-level intrusions. The intrusive and seismic

Figure 5 Yr Elen. Mudstones in the upper part of the Nant Ffrancon Formation. (L2545)

8

activity heralded the onset of a major episode of volcanism. Within the Nant Ffrancon Formation the only expression of extrusive volcanism is a thin manganiferous basic tuff exposed in the north of the district.

The Nant Ffrancon Formation has yielded fossils from only a few scattered localities and a detailed biostratigraphic subdivision has proved impossible. Acritarchs of Arenig and Llanvirn ages are found in the lower part of the formation. In the west the mudstones are graptolitic and have yielded faunas of Arenig to Caradoc ages. Greenly (1944, p.77) listed faunas from the Arenig, lower Llanvirn and Llandeilo and our survey has revealed an upper Llanvirn fauna near Caernarfon. Also a lower Caradoc fauna was found, in beds probably near the top of the formation, on Penrhyn Castle foreshore: it includes *Amplexograptus arctus?*, *Climacograptus bicornis* (group), *Dicellograptus* sp., *Dicranograptus rectus*, *Lasiograptus costatus* and *Orthograptus* cf. *apiculatus*, and indicates a low level in the *multidens* Zone. To the east, the few graptolites from around Foel-fras have not proved of stratigraphic value, but to the south Llanvirn graptolites occur in Cwm Dudodyn (Williams, 1930, p.199) and beds near the top of the formation north of Y Garn yielded Caradocian graptolites, low in the *multidens* Zone. The formation thus extends from the Arenig to the lower Caradoc.

Localities: Slopes on the west side of the Pass of Nant Ffrancon [635 620], *Penrhyn foreshore* [604 731].

LLEWELYN VOLCANIC GROUP

The group marks the first major phase of Caradoc volcanism in northern Snowdonia (Howells and others, 1983). The activity developed at a number of volcanic centres, in part penecontemporaneous, which produced both petrographically distinct and mixed formations. These formations, together with the associated sediments, constitute the Llewelyn Volcanic Group. The sequence from the base of the Llewelyn Volcanic Group to above the Dolgarrog Volcanic Formation falls within one extended graptolite zone, of *Diplograptus multidens*, and corresponds to part of the Soudleyan and much of the Longvillian.

Only the Capel Curig Volcanic Formation, the highest of the constituent formations, extends along the full outcrop; in south-eastern Snowdonia it is the sole representative of the Group. The underlying formations are more local, and are described below in their occurrence from north-east to south-west.

Conwy Rhyolite Formation (CoR) The Conwy Rhyolite Formation extends south-westwards from Conwy, north of the district, to beyond Afon Anafon. It is thickest to the north of Tal y Fan. It is composed of thick rhyolite lavas and interflow breccias with intercalated tuffs and sediments which are more prominent in the south-west of the outcrop.

The rhyolites were probably extruded from a centre lying to the north of the Bangor district near Conwy, where they are intruded by a late-stage rhyolite plug. Away from this centre uniform siltstones are increasingly to be found intercalated within the thick pile of rhyolite flows, and this, together with the lack of clear erosional breaks, suggests that the formation was subaqueously emplaced.
Locality: Cefn Coch [726 746].

Foel Fras Volcanic Complex (FfV) The complex is a thick accumulation of lavas and associated late-stage intrusions of intermediate composition, best developed about the area of Foel Fras. The disposition of the intrusive and extrusive rocks close to Foel Fras suggests that a volcanic centre lay here, and possibly took the form of a small caldera. To the north, near Afon Anafon and Bera Mawr (Figure 6), the complex abuts against the Conwy Rhyolite Formation, and locally interdigitates with it, indicating that the two types of volcanism were active at the same time. To the south, tuff and flow-banded lava, which escaped from the centre, can be traced to the north side of the Nant Ffrancon Pass. An ash-flow tuff in this sequence is welded in the north and passes laterally into non-welded tuffs to the south. Some associated bedded tuffs in the south may have been produced by sloughing of material from the non-welded top of the ash-flow. Another associated tuff, of limited extent, crops out in the north, above the Conwy Rhyolite Formation.
Localities: Bera Bach [672 677] *and Foel-fras* [698 682].

Foel Grach Basalt Formation (FgB) The formation comprises two distinct accumulations of basaltic rocks, one on Carnedd Llewelyn and the other about the Nant Ffrancon Pass. At Carnedd Llewelyn the formation lies at the base of the Llewelyn Volcanic Group, and forms a broad dome-like accumulation of basalts and basaltic breccias with little indication of individual flows or interdigitated sediments. About the Nant Ffrancon Pass, it consists of basalt flows interbedded with marine sediments, and passing laterally into them.

Typically the basalts are grey-green and show a markedly variable abundance of feldspar phenocrysts and amygdales. The original mineralogy has been altered, probably by reaction with sea water, by low-grade regional metamorphism, and by surface weathering. The original calcic plagioclase has been altered to albite, and the original

Figure 6 Bera Mawr. Tor of quartz latite of the Foel Fras Volcanic Complex. (L1927)

ferromagnesian minerals (probably mainly augite) to chlorite, clinozoisite, actinolite and carbonate.

Basaltic breccias occur throughout the thick sequence on Carnedd Llewelyn and at the top and bottom of the well-defined flows about Nant Ffrancon. Pillow forms are rare, and the basalt blocks are generally sub-angular. Columnar joints are locally well developed in the massive central portions of the flows.

At Carnedd Llewelyn, the dome-like accumulation of basalt and basaltic breccias suggests that this was the site of a short-lived volcanic centre which was little eroded in the rapidly subsiding basin before it was covered by sediments.

Locality: Carnedd Llewelyn [684 645].

Braich tu du Volcanic Formation (BDT) The formation is hybrid in its petrographic types and lithological characters. It comprises rhyolite flows, acidic ash-flow tuff, basic tuff and tuffite, but no single horizon persists across the whole outcrop. It extends from north of Nant Peris to Carnedd Llewelyn and Foel Grach, and is most clearly defined on the Braich tu du ridge to the north of the Pass of Nant Ffrancon.

At Braich tu du the sequence is dominated by two thick rhyolite flows, one above and one below a welded acidic ash-flow tuff with basalt, basic tuffs and sediments. The welding in the ash-flow tuff is intense, and the fabric has been distorted by internal stress within the flow, possibly by movement of entrapped water vapour and volatiles following its emplacement. The rhyolites show even and contorted flow banding, autobrecciation (particularly at the top and bottom of the flows), siliceous nodules and columnar joints.

The variation in thickness and the lateral impersistence of the horizons result from penecontemporaneous faulting. These movements were most intense early in the volcanism, but continued throughout.

South of the Pass of Nant Ffrancon, between the flanks of Y Garn and Nant Peris, the main members of the formation pass laterally into reworked acid tuffs, basic tuffs and marine sediments, and this passage supports the interpretation that the formation was emplaced in water.

10 *Locality: Braich tu du ridge* [652 626].

Strata below Capel Curig Volcanic Formation The strata, mostly sedimentary, that underlie the Capel Curig Volcanic Formation are a variable assemblage which have not been given a formational name. They are well defined in the Tryfan Anticline where the outcrop of the Capel Curig Volcanic Formation closes to the south of the Ogwen Valley. In the core of the anticline there is a thick sequence of siltstones, sandstones, tuffites and acid tuffs, all of which lie within the Llewelyn Volcanic Group. Close to the middle of this sequence is an acid tuff called the Gwern Gof Tuff. This tuff links the sequence of the Tryfan Anticline with the main succession at Bwlch Cyffryw

Figure 7 West-facing flank of Tryfan viewed across Llyn Bochlwyd. The top of the Capel Curig Volcanic Formation forms the feature high on the slope. The Pitts Head Tuff outcrops in the promontory on the far side of the lake. (L1911)

Figure 8 Ffynnon Llugwy. Craig yr Ysfa ridge to left on which the Capel Curig Volcanic Formation crops out. (L2542)

Drum where it lies closely above the Foel Fras Volcanic Complex. In the Tryfan Anticline the character of the bedding of the sandstones and siltstones underlying the tuff points to a shallow marine environment which was subject to tidal action (Howells and others, in press). This view is supported by the fossils which, although often poorly preserved, have a Soudleyan aspect. They are mostly brachiopods: *Bicuspina, Dalmanella, Dinorthis, Howellites, Macrocoelia* and *Rostricellula.*

The Gwern Gof Tuff is a thick massive acidic ash-flow tuff overlain by bedded reworked tuffs. The ash-flow tuff is locally welded, although in the main it is non-welded. The overlying bedded tuffs represent the reworked top of the underlying ash-flow tuff. The strata between the Gwern Gof Tuff and the base of the Capel Curig Volcanic Formation are sandstones and siltstones.

About Bwlch y Ddeufaen the sequence is almost entirely composed of heterolithic pebble conglomerates with sandstones, which have been interpreted as alluvial fan-base, sheet-flood deposits (Howells and Leveridge, 1980). South and east of Bwlch y Ddeufaen the sequence thickens markedly. Here the strata reflect a changing environment, through a zone showing interaction between standing-water and fluvial deposition about the Ogwen Valley to offshore-marine conditions south-east of Capel Curig (Howells and Leveridge, 1980). The determining factor which controlled this variation in thickness and lithology is thought to have been an active hinge-line, aligned NE–SW, close to Craig yr Ysfa, that possibly marks the line of a concealed basement fracture.

Localities: Bwlch y Ddeufaen [710 718], *Tryfan Fach* [665 602].

Capel Curig Volcanic Formation (CCV) This uppermost formation of the Llewelyn Volcanic Group represents one of the major episodes of Caradoc acid volcanism in north-east Snowdonia. The formation can be traced from Conwy, beyond the district in the northeast, through the eastern flank of the Carneddau, to beyond Capel Curig in the south-east. It is nowhere more dramatically exposed than on Tryfan (Figure 7) (Howells and Leveridge, 1980).

The volcanism was predominantly of ash-flow type, and originated in three separate volcanic centres which were in part contemporaneous. North of Craig yr Ysfa (Figure 8) the formation is represented by a continuous sequence of ash-flow tuffs, whereas to the south this sequence is broken by intercalated sediments with prolific and varied faunas characteristic of a nearshore, high-energy environment, rich in brachiopods, molluscs and trilobites. The lowest two ash-flows were erupted from a centre in the north, and extended eastwards and southwards into the sea. To the south, the transition from subaerial to subaqueous conditions occurred close to Craig yr Ysfa. These tuffs are typically strongly welded, although variations are recognised which can be related to the changing emplacement environment. Where deposition was subaerial the bases of the ash-flow tuffs are even and non-welded; where it was beneath water the tuffs 11 have collapsed into the underlying sediments, producing extremely irregular bases, and the tuffs are welded to the contact (Francis and Howells, 1973). Following the eruption of the lowest ash-flow, subsidence to the south of the initial land area produced a northward marine transgression, and an eruptive centre developed in the vicinity of Glyder Fach. Subsequent activity was restricted to small ash-flows from a subaerial vent probably in the vicinity of Yr Elen and to the Glyder Fach centre. The character and distribution of the pyroclastics about Glyder Fach and their relationship with the associated sediments indicate that deposition around this centre was clearly influenced by a marine environment. However, the common occurrence of accretionary lapilli tuffs is evidence that the eruption column itself was subaerial.

Localities: Craig yr Ysfa [692 642], *Gallt yr Ogof* [693 597].

Cwm Eigiau Formation (CEi) The Cwm Eigiau Formation lies between the top of the Llewelyn Volcanic Group and the base of the Snowdon Volcanic Group. It is dominated by siltstones and sandstones although fine-grained air-fall dust-tuffs and local accumulations of basalts and basaltic tuffs attest to continued, but restricted, volcanism.

Within the formation there is clear evidence of the continuing influence on sedimentation of the active hinge-line near Craig yr Ysfa. To the north of the hinge-line, in the Tal y Fan area, the formation comprises about 450 m of shallow-water sandstones whereas to the south and east of Ffynnon Llugwy it thickens to about 1300 m of deeper-water mudstones and siltstones with fairly persistent sandstone beds, which include beds of air-fall dust-tuffs in the middle of the sequence (Howells and others, 1978, 1981). These sandstones are fossiliferous and form a prominent feature about Capel Curig. The faunas, mainly brachiopods (notably *Plaesiomys multifida*) and trilobites (especially *Broeggerolithus nicholsoni*), are of late Soudleyan to early Longvillian age.

Between the passes of Llanberis and Nant Ffrancon, the Pitts Head Tuff, associated with shallow-water fossiliferous sandstones, occurs near the top of the formation (Howells and others, in press). It is an acidic ash-flow tuff which was erupted from a centre at Llwyd Mawr in south-west Snowdonia (Roberts, 1967); its thickness is fairly uniform and its distinctive petrographic character continues to the southern flank of Pen yr ole Wen. The overlying sandstones include beds of air-fall water-settled dust-tuffs well exposed in Cwm Idwal and the Pass of Llanberis where they were formerly quarried for honestones. In the Idwal area, the faunas above the Pitts Head Tuff include numerous brachiopods, such as *Plaesiomys multifida* and *Sowerbyella soudleyensis*, which suggest a transition from a late Soudleyan to early Longvillian age, while in the Llanberis Pass the equivalent rocks contain the brachiopods *Dinorthis berwynensis* and *Macrocoelia expansa*, which are less diagnostic of precise age but clearly indicative of a shallow-water high-energy environment.

At the top of the formation, both on the east flank of the Idwal Syncline and in the Pass of Llanberis, local basalt flows and piles of basaltic breccias underlie the Lower Rhyolitic Tuff Formation.

Localities: North-east of Capel Curig [724 586], *Pont y Gromlech* [628 564] *including Pitts Head Tuff.*

SNOWDON VOLCANIC GROUP

The Snowdon Volcanic Group (Howells and others, 1983) is broadly equivalent to the Snowdon Volcanic 'Suite' as defined by Williams (1927). Its usage has been extended to include equivalent strata to the north-west previously designated as the Crafnant Volcanic Group, synonymous with the 'Crafnant Volcanic Series' (Davies, 1936) of the Trefriw area. Rocks of the group form most of the Snowdon massif south of the Pass of Llanberis, where it has been divided in upward succession into the Lower Rhyolitic Tuff Formation, the Bedded Pyroclastic Formation and the Upper Rhyolitic Tuff Formation. Only the lower two of these formations crop out in the Bangor district, in the Idwal syncline extending northwards to Cwm Idwal (Figure 9). In the Trefriw area the group has been divided into the Lower, Middle and Upper Crafnant Volcanic Formations (Howells and others, 1971). The Lower Crafnant Volcanic Formation has been correlated in some detail with the Lower Rhyolitic Tuff Formation of Dolwyddelan,

Figure 9 Panoramic view to south side of Llyn Ogwen. Tryfan ridge to left, Glyder Fach, Glyder Fawr, Cwm Idwal, Y Garn to right exposing a section through the Idwal Syncline, from the Capel Curig Volcanic Formation on Tryfan to the Bedded Pyroclastic Formation in the cliffs at the back of Cwm Idwal. (L2391, L2390)

which lies to the south of the Bangor district (Howells and others, 1973), and extends from there to central Snowdonia. The Bedded Pyroclastic Formation in the central area is broadly equivalent to the Middle Crafnant Volcanic Formation in the east.

Lower Rhyolitic Tuff Formation (LR) The base of the formation is exposed at Dinas y Gromlech on the north side of the Pass of Llanberis. It is taken at the base of a coarse pyroclastic breccia which grades up into an acidic ash-flow tuff. The breccia includes blocks of acidic tuff, sandstone, and locally numerous vesiculated basalt blocks. The breccia conformably overlies acid air-fall dust-tuffs at Dinas y Gromlech, although southwards and northwards it transgresses the

underlying sediments to come into juxtaposition with the Pitts Head Tuff (Howells and others, in press).

On the south side of the Pass of Llanberis the formation comprises thick uniform ash-flow tuffs with little indication of bedding surfaces. Immediately north of the Pass, there are some signs of bedding above the thick basal ash-flow tuff, with intercalation of siltstone and basic tuff and, at the top, a thick rhyolite flow which is exposed on Esgair Felen (Figure 10). The bedding becomes generally better defined northwards and is particularly evident in Cwm Idwal.

In Cwm Idwal the basal pyroclastic breccia is well exposed below the Idwal Slabs on the east flank of the syncline. It grades up into primary acidic ash-flow tuffs, which in turn grade up into tuffs that **13**

Figure 10 Llanberis Pass. Esgair Felen, at top of ridge to the right, is in rhyolite near the top of the Lower Rhyolitic Tuff formation. Llyn Padarn in distance. (L2568)

have characters indicative of secondary emplacement by mass flow or reworking of previously deposited pyroclastic debris. A thick sequence of siltstones, locally tuffaceous, with few sandstone and tuff beds occurs below the rhyolite that is exposed in the cliffs below Twll Du [639 588]. The faunas in this area are not well preserved, but the presence of the brachiopod *Sericoidea,* associated with trinucleid trilobites, suggests a quieter and deeper-water environment than that of the underlying Cwm Eigiau Formation. The rhyolite is overlain by massive beds of ash-flow tuffs with flaggy reworked tops. On the slopes of Glyder Fawr to the south-west on the east flank of the syncline, these tuffs overlap on to the upper surface of the rhyolite.

The formation is thickest south of the Pass of Llanberis, where it overlies shallow-water marine sandstones and is overlain by marine emplaced basalts, hyaloclastites and basaltic tuffs with intercalated siltstones. For such a thick pile of acidic ash-flow tuffs to have been accommodated with no indication of erosion there must have been considerable subsidence, possibly fault controlled. The way in which the Lower Rhyolitic Tuff Formation changes character and becomes thinner northward from south of the Pass of Llanberis indicates a change from proximal to distal accumulation. Also to the north, the presence of slumped ash-flow tuffs and intercalated marine sediments between primary ash-flow tuffs and rhyolite indicates subaqueous accumulation away from the centre of eruption.
Localities: Idwal Slabs [646 587], *Dinas y Gromlech, Pass of Llanberis* [630 569].

Bedded Pyroclastic Formation (BP) The Bedded Pyroclastic Formation is exposed in the core of the Idwal Syncline (Figure 9) between Nant Peris and Cwm Idwal. It comprises basalt, basaltic breccias and well-bedded basic tuffs. At Twll Du, in the back wall of Cwm Idwal, bedded coarse- and fine-grained basic tuffs, which show grading, cross-bedding and ripple-marked surfaces, occur at the base of the formation. The tuffs are locally fossiliferous (Dean, 1965; Howells and others, in press), the faunas, including *Chasmops cambrensis* and *Nicolella actoniae obesa,* being indicative of a Longvillian age. The tuffs are overlain by a thick pile of basaltic pillow breccias. Above the Cwm these breccias are overlain by bedded basic tuffs and basalt flows.

Southwards towards Nant Peris, the bedded character persists along strike, although locally, as in the crags to the south-east of Pistyll Gwyn, there is a thick pile of unbedded fragmented basaltic breccia and hyaloclastite. This pile possibly represents an eruptive centre, although the contact between this accumulation and the bedded tuffs is not exposed.

The nature of the bedding within the tuffs and the faunas that are included lead to the inference that the formation was emplaced in a shallow marine environment. Many of the coarse- and fine-grained alternations in the tuffs probably represent both variations in the erupted materials and sedimentary reworking and sorting.
Locality: Twll Du, Cwm Idwal [639 588].

Lower Crafnant Volcanic Formation (LCV) Around Capel Curig the formation is composed of three major tuffs numbered 1 to 3 (Howells and others, 1978), although to the north of Llyn Cowlyd an intervening tuff (No. 2a) is present (Howells and others, 1981) and thickens northwards. The tuffs are interbedded with marine sediments and form prominent scarps.

The tuffs are typical products of ash-flow tuff eruptions with varying proportions of shards, feldspar crystals, pumice clasts, lithic clasts and matrix. In the basal zone of the tuffs, as in the No. 1 Tuff at Capel Curig (Howells and others, 1973), fragmented and complete brachiopod shells occur, providing persuasive evidence that the flows were emplaced on a marine depositional slope. Apart from one locality of the No. 1 Tuff at Pen y Castell (Howells and others, 1981), the tuffs of the formation are non-welded.

The three tuffs show contrasting lithological characters, although each flow is in itself remarkably uniform. They can be traced from the Conwy area, north of the Bangor district, to Betws-y-Coed in the south-east, and their outcrops pick out the structure clearly. Howells and others (1973) argued that the No. 1 and No. 2 tuffs represent the distal parts of primary ash-flow tuff eruptions from the volcanic centre of the Lower Rhyolitic Tuff Formation in central Snowdonia. However it is now believed that only the No. 1 tuff was erupted from that centre. The distinctive coarse clast-rich lithology and the distribution of the No. 3 Tuff seem to represent a more proximal part of an ash-flow emanating from a centre in the country around Crafnant.

Locality: East of Capel Curig village [727 576].

Middle Crafnant Volcanic Formation (MCV) The formation can be recognised as a distinct unit only in a restricted area to the south-east of the Crafnant Valley, most typically about Sarnau, north-west of Betws-y-Coed (Howells and others, 1978). It comprises well-bedded alternations of acid tuffs, tuffites, and sediments. The tuffs include thin blocky ash-flow tuffs and light grey, fine-grained air-fall water-settled dust-tuffs. The sediments are typically fine-grained, blue-black, graptolitic mudstones and siltstones with a few thin beds of turbiditic sandstone, which suggest accumulation in deep water.

The fauna includes *Amplexograptus arctus, A. fallax* and species of *Climacograptus, Glyptograptus* and *Orthograptus*.

In the Sarnau area the tuffs and sediments alternate regularly. The dust-tuffs are commonly striped with bluish-black mudstone bands, which formed during pauses in the settlement of the fine ash into the water. The striped beds are commonly convoluted, as a result of unequal and rapid loading by an overlying blocky ash-flow tuff, or by seismic shock (Howells and others, 1978). Westwards from Sarnau to the area north-east of Capel Curig, this evenly bedded sequence passes laterally into slumped sequences, probably along the margin of an unstable volcanic pile. The slumped sequence extends northwards to the Crafnant valley, beyond which the Middle and Upper Crafnant Volcanic formations cannot be separated; in consequence the two have here been mapped as a single unit.

Locality: Sarnau, near Betws-y-Coed [775 588].

Upper Crafnant Volcanic Formation (UCV) The formation is broadly equivalent to the Upper Tuff 'Bed' of Davies (1936). It can be most clearly defined in the Gwydir Forest north-west of Betws-y-Coed (Howells and others, 1978). It is a thick bluish-grey massive tuffite almost entirely without internal bedding. The tuffite is a heterogeneous mixture of cuspate shards, pumice fragments, feldspar crystals and lithic clasts set in a mudstone matrix. The proportions of the constituents are highly variable. The pyroclastic components are typical products of ash-flow eruptions. The complete lack of sorting and minimal internal bedding in the formation suggest that the tuffite was deposited by a high-density gravity flow, produced by the remobilisation of previously deposited pyroclastic debris and unlithified mud.

In places, towards the top of the formation, the tuffite is finer and grades upwards into tuffaceous mudstone.

Locality: Mynydd Bwlch yr Haiarn, south-west of Llanwrst [777 587].

Undivided Middle and Upper Crafnant Volcanic formations (M/UCV) North of the Crafnant valley the mudstone matrix in the tuffite of the Upper Crafnant Volcanic Formation becomes much less abundant, and the tuffite passes into an acidic tuff similar to those in the Middle Crafnant Volcanic Formation. The two formations then cannot be told apart.

Generally the undivided unit is a chaotic mixture of acid tuff, tuffite, siltstone and mudstone; it runs the gamut from slumped discrete beds to rocks in which the pyroclastic and epiclastic elements are completely mixed together. Any undisturbed bedding is laterally impersistent. North-west of Dolgarrog the formation is some 1000 m thick, which suggests that it accumulated near its source. The thinner and divided formations to the south are also consistent with this interpretation.
Locality: Moel Eilio [745 659].

The relationship between the Middle Crafnant Volcanic Formation in eastern Snowdonia and the Bedded Pyroclastic Formation in central Snowdonia bears on the environmental interpretation. The two formations are sharply contrasted: deep-water mudstones with associated acidic volcanics in the eastern area; and basaltic volcanics reworked in shallow water in the central area. It has been suggested (Howells, 1977) that the two areas were separated by a rising ridge which formed a barrier between the environments of deposition and which was also the source area of the turbiditic sandstones which occur in the Middle Crafnant Volcanic Formation north-west of Betws-y-Coed.

Tal y Fan Volcanic Formation (TF) The formation is restricted to Tal y Fan [742 730]. It comprises basalts, hyaloclastites, basaltic breccias and basic tuffs, with locally intercalated siltstones and mudstones. There are acidic ash-flow tuffs of the Snowdon Volcanic Group below and within the formation which indicate that the formation was deposited, in part at least, contemporaneously with the acid tuffs.

The formation is intruded by thick dolerite sills thought to be high-level intrusions into unlithified water-saturated sediments. Locally the sills pass laterally into basalts, hyaloclastites and basic tuffs, becoming extrusive rather than intrusive. Hyaloclastites and pillowed basalts within the formation are associated with marine sediments, thus indicating subaqueous deposition. The basaltic rocks are limited in extent and have been reworked only slightly, which suggests that the water was deep. The fact that a particular acidic ash-flow tuff can be traced through the Tal y Fan Volcanic Formation indicates that the volcanic rocks had little topographic expression when the tuff was deposited. The basaltic rocks presumably accumulated in a depression which subsided at a rate just sufficient to accommodate them, and yet allowed a distal acidic ash-flow tuff to be emplaced across them.
Locality: Tal y Fan [742 730].

Dolgarrog Volcanic Formation (DV) The Dolgarrog Volcanic Formation overlies the Snowdon Volcanic Group to the west of Dolgarrog. The formation comprises massive hyaloclastites, pillow breccias, basalts and basaltic tuffs, with no subdivisions persistent enough to be mappable (Howells and others, 1981). It is the product of submarine basaltic eruptions, transgressive bodies of dolerite at the base and within the formation representing feeders. The developing pile was unstable: continuing eruptions caused it to collapse at the edges and the resulting basaltic debris was deposited as thin graded beds.

The formation is similar to the Tal y Fan Volcanic Formation but has been excluded from the Snowdon Volcanic Group. As in the Tal y Fan Volcanic Formation the volcanics have been reworked only slightly, and little basaltic debris has been incorporated in the overlying mudstones. These factors, together with evidence from the basaltic components indicate that the formation accumulated in water sufficiently deep for the rocks to remain submerged and so not be eroded on a large scale.
Locality: Pont Newydd, Afon Porth-llwyd [759 670].

Cadnant Shales (= **Llanrhychwyn Slates**) (CaS) The Cadnant Shales overlie the Snowdon Volcanic Group and, locally, the Dolgarrog Volcanic Formation, with very little evidence that the volcanics have been reworked. They are predominantly black, pyritic and well cleaved, and are best exposed on Cefn Cyfarwydd on the north side of the Crafnant Valley. They were first defined by Elles (1909) working in the Conwy area, just to the north of the district, where they overlie the Tal y Fan Volcanic Formation. In the north-east they are generally less well cleaved than elsewhere in the district, where they were previously named the Llanrhychwyn Slates. Graptolite faunas collected during our survey have been assigned to the *Diplograptus multidens* Zone, but the record of *Dicranograptus clingani* in the Dolwyddelan area, to the south of the district, suggests the presence also of part of the overlying *D. clingani* Zone (Williams and Bulman, 1931).

The Cadnant Shales overlie beds at least as young as Upper Longvillian, but at this stratigraphic level beds of similar lithology extend over a wide area of the Welsh Basin (Cave, 1965) and in the Welshpool area have yielded trilobites of the Onnian stage at the top of the Caradoc. Williams and Bulman (1931) assumed that the mudstones were deposited in shallow water because they overlie tuffs that they thought accumulated in shallow water. Howells and others (1978, 1981) argue that there is no firm evidence to suggest that the Upper Crafnant Volcanic Formation was emplaced in shallow water, and suggest that the deep water black mudstone environment, which was established during the deposition of the Middle Crafnant Volcanic Formation, continued.
Locality: Pen y Ffridd Quarry [774 609].

Trefriw Tuff (TrT) South of the Crafnant valley, greyish black mudstones with impersistent sandstone intercalations lie at the top of the Cadnant Shales; locally, as to the south of Trefriw, the sandstones are markedly more abundant. Northwards these strata pass laterally into basaltic tuffs with agglomeratic bands and siltstone partings, and are separately identified on the map as the Trefriw Tuff.

The lithologies and sedimentary structures of the Trefriw Tuff indicate it was formed by the reworking of basic volcanics in shallow water. The facies variations suggest that the source of the eruptions was in the Dolgarrog area, and that the tuff probably represents a resurgence of activity from the volcanic centre which gave rise to the Dolgarrog Volcanic Formation. The southward transition through sandstones to mudstone suggests sedimentary reworking close to the centre, probably a result of local uplift. To the north, near Llanbedr y cennin, the Trefriw Tuff cannot be distinguished.
Locality: Berth-llwyd [776 648].

Conwy Mudstone (= Grinllwm Slates) (CyM) These mostly grey mudstones are the youngest Ordovician rocks in the Bangor district. They overlie the Trefriw Tuff and, elsewhere, the Cadnant Shales. North-east from Tal y Fan the Conwy Mudstone extends into the Conwy area (Elles, 1909) where a prominent sandstone occurs near the top of the formation. Elles considered that the basal part of these mudstones was Caradoc in age while the rest was Ashgill. More recently, it has been indicated (Price, 1977; Campbell, 1983) that the entire formation is Ashgill.

South of Tal y Fan they were previously termed the Grinllwm Slates (Davies, 1936); they are well exposed along the escarpment below Gwydir High Park, south of Llanrwst. They are composed of grey mudstone and siltstone, with thin flaggy bands of cross-bedded sandstone that show ripple-marked surfaces. Northwards, as on Grinllwm, sandstones are less common. Between Tal-y-Bont and Llanbedr y cennin, numerous small exposures of grey silty mudstone show bioturbation structures, and Stevenson (1971) recorded a shelly fauna in the vicinity.
Locality: Gwydir High Park [795 608].

The Conwy Valley Fault divides the outcrops of the Ordovician rocks in the west from those of the Silurian in the east. Along much of its outcrop the fault is obscured by thick drift in the floor of the Conwy valley. The Silurian of the Bangor district forms a western extension of outcrops that form much of the county of Clwyd (Warren and others, 1984). The rocks are mainly mudstones, siltstones and sandstones which, in parts of the sequence, are variably slumped. They were deposited in an east–west basin bounded on its west side by a landmass of uplifted Ordovician rocks. The sedimentation was affected by penecontemporaneous movements on the Conwy Valley Fault.

In comparison with the underlying Ordovician, the Silurian strata are richly fossiliferous. They contain shelly faunas and, more significantly, graptolites which allow detailed biostratigraphic subdivision of the sequence (Warren and others, 1984).

Bryn Dowsi Mudstone and Pale Slates (BDo, PSl) The lowest Silurian (Llandovery) rocks are the dark grey Bryn Dowsi Mudstones.

They are graptolitic, bioturbated and generally have been deposited in a quiescent, shallow marine environment. They comprise the lower part of the Gyffin Shales of Elles (1909) and are overlain by paler coloured mudstones, the Pale Slates.

Denbigh Grits (DG) The overlying Denbigh Grits are of early Wenlock age, comprising sandstones and mudstones deposited from turbidity currents flowing into deeper parts of the basin. Many of these beds subsequently slumped or were fragmented in situ, probably as a result of seismic shocks; many of the 'disturbed beds' are the products of these processes. Characteristically the formation shows rapid lateral lithological variations.

Lower Nantglyn Flags (LNF) The uppermost Silurian strata in the Bangor district belong to the Lower Nantglyn Flags (Warren and others, 1984). These are mudstones and laminated muddy siltstones, with a few thin lenticular bands of calcareous siltstone. Individual beds are remarkably persistent over a wide area. The sequence includes several 'disturbed beds' of mudstone and siltstone.
Localities: Old quarry near Llanrwst [7986 6302] *and crags near Maenan* [7996 6591].

5 Carboniferous rocks

Carboniferous rocks are confined to an area between the Dinorwic Fault and the Menai Straits. They lie unconformably on Ordovician (Arenig) cleaved mudstones. The sequence includes Dinantian (Viséan) formations (George and others, 1976), which are unconformably overlain by red measures of supposed Westphalian age (George, 1974; Calver and Smith, 1974).

Menai Straits Formation (MiF) Assorted lithologies within the lowermost strata make up the Menai Straits Formation. The sequence records a lateral transition from a terrestrial to a marginal marine (paralic) environment. Close to Britannia Bridge, basal loams are overlain by coarse fluvial sandstones derived from the south-west. North-eastwards these interdigitate with seat-earths, carbonaceous and bioclastic mudstones, and caliche and bioclastic limestones. There is an upward gradation into the Treborth Formation.

The formation corresponds with the Loam Breccia Formation and the Basement Series of Greenly (1928, p.419). Miospore evidence (Hibbert and Lacey 1969, p.437) indicates a Holkerian or Asbian age for the Basement Series (George and others 1976, p.32).
Locality: Close to Brittania Bridge [543 710].

Treborth Formation (TrF) The formation consists of thin- and thick-bedded shelly limestones and thin marine shales. Many of the included corals occur in growth positions. Incursions of fluvial sandstones locally fill deep channels, as at Gored y Gut, and reflect a continuing terrestrial influence on the sediments.

Smith *in* Greenly (1928, p.402) listed the coral-brachiopod faunas from these beds, which he referred to the D_1, D_2, and D_3 subzones. The assemblages are typical of the Asbian and Brigantian stages, (George and others, 1976, p.34).
Locality: Shoreline, Gored y Gut [572 725].

Dinorwic Formation (DcF) The formation contrasts sharply with the underlying one. It is characterised by white-weathering cherts and by beds of locally brecciated dolomitic limestone, interbedded with a few thin, laterally impersistent, sandstones. There is evidence that sediment was transported parallel to the confining faults, which suggests deposition in a cuvette, though the absence of coarse clastics adjacent to the Dinorwic Fault suggests that the margins were gentle and inactive.

No diagnostic fauna is noted from this formation (which is equivalent to the Chert Series of Greenly) in the Bangor area (Greenly, 1928, p.402), but farther to the east, near Prestatyn, fossils indicate a late Brigantian age (George and others, 1976, fig. 9:5).

The Dinantian rocks were affected by substantial earth movements (see p.25) and erosion before the deposition of the remainder of the Carboniferous sequence.
Locality: near Port Dinorwic [519 672]

Plas Brereton Formation (PBF) The formation crops out in a small area adjacent to the Menai Straits, south-east of Port Dinorwic. It consists of red measures which, within the district, mainly comprise coarse conglomerates with thin bands of soft red sandstone and mudstone. The conglomerates contain pebble- and cobble-size clasts in a friable clay matrix. Clasts are variable, with Lower Palaeozoic sedimentary rocks and intrusive and extrusive volcanic rocks forming distinctive components. The formation lies with marked unconformity on the Dinorwic Formation. It was termed the Red Measures by Greenly (1938), and it is referred to the Westphalian mainly on lithological grounds (Calver and Smith, 1974).

The Plas Brereton Formation comprehensively buried a deeply dissected topography cut in the underlying Dinorwic Formation. This and its red colour suggest that it was deposited subaerially and rapidly. Possibly the dominant process was influxes of alluvial debris marginal to the active Dinorwic Fault, with subordinate phases of fluvial influence. The conglomerates are less important in the higher parts of the formation, and this suggests that the fault became less active and topography therefore less marked, so that low-profile fluvial deposition ensued. Temporary shallow lakes may have formed.
Locality: near Llanfair Hall [512 662].

6   Intrusive igneous rocks

Intrusions of Lower Palaeozoic age form a distinctive component of the geology of the Bangor district. They can be broadly divided into two main types, acid and basic, although a few of intermediate composition also occur. The form and distribution of the intrusions allow another generalisation to be made: boss-like intrusions of intermediate or granitoid composition occur near the base and below the main outcrop of Caradoc volcanics; transgressive thick dolerite sills and bodies of intrusive rhyolite are, to a large extent, restricted to the outcrop of the Caradoc volcanics. Information on the geochemistry of the intrusions is sparse, and classification of the rock types has been based on petrography.

The oldest intrusion in the district is a granite within the Padarn Tuff Formation on the Bangor ridge, south of Port Dinorwic. This is part of the Twt Hill intrusion and has been dated at 498 ± 7 million years. The granite is unconformably overlain by basal Ordovician sediments. Several small and large boss-like intrusions of diorite to granite composition, of Caradocian age, lie generally along a NNE–SSW line from the Penmaenmawr intrusion at the northern edge of the district to the Bwlch y Cywion intrusion south of Nant Ffrancon [640 605]. Apparently small bodies of microdiorite to the south of the Penmaenmawr intrusion are identical to the marginal facies of the main intrusion, and it is probable they are connected to it

at depth. The Bwlch y Cywion microgranite includes a late intrusive phase of rhyolite which transgresses locally into the adjacent sediments. The intrusion produces a broad metamorphic aureole which can be clearly defined along most of its outcrop. The marginal facies of the Ogwen microgranite [655 607] is also composed of flow-banded rhyolite, although there is no indication that this reflects a separate late intrusive phase.

Most commonly the rhyolite intrusions are closely associated with the extrusive volcanic rocks. This is true of those occurring in the Lower Rhyolitic Tuff Formation about the Pass of Llanberis. These are late-stage intrusions into the extrusive volcanic pile, and commonly have dome-like forms. Locally these intrusive rhyolites extend into an extrusive phase. The rhyolite south-west of Nant Peris [610 580] was previously considered to be extrusive (Talgau lavas of Williams, 1930), but recent mapping has demonstrated that it intrudes sediments of the Nant Ffrancon Formation.

The Lower Palaeozoic dolerites mainly occur as transgressive sills, for example at Cwm Eigiau [715 644]; they are almost all intimately associated with the Caradocian volcanic rocks. There is clear evidence that they were folded along with the associated strata, and all the intrusions have been affected to some extent by cleavage. On this evidence, it seems that they are part of the Ordovician magmatic episode rather than an intrusive event associated with the Caledonian earth movements at the end of the Silurian (Howells and others, 1981). Many of the intrusions are extremely thick and in places they have a coarse-grained gabbroic texture.

The only younger intrusive rocks in the district are a few thin basaltic dykes of Tertiary age which intrude Cambrian, Ordovician and Carboniferous strata.

Quaternary deposits

During the Quaternary, North Wales was subjected to severe glaciations which moulded the landscape to its present form. Evidence of the erosional effects of the ice is nowhere more dramatically displayed than in the high ridges and cwms of the Glyders and the Carneddau. Throughout the Quaternary, cold phases, some producing land ice, were interspersed with warmer episodes; but much of the evidence of the earlier glacial and interglacial phases has been removed by the most recent, late Devensian, glaciation, which left extensive deposits. The glacial chronology of the region has been summarised by Whittow and Ball (1970).

At its maximum the Devensian ice-sheet in North Wales is thought to have been centred on an inland plateau to the east of Snowdonia: it is referred to as the Merioneth Ice Cap. The ice-cap extended to the North Wales coast where it abutted against an ice-sheet referred to as the Irish Sea Ice. The Irish Sea Ice moved south-westwards along the coast, in places extending a short distance up the main valleys, such as the Conwy valley. At a late stage in the glaciation the mainland ice retreated, first to isolated centres such as the Glyders and Carneddau, and ultimately, about 10 000 years ago, to the innermost recesses of the high cwms, before finally melting.

The valleys of Nant Ffrancon and Llanberis, with their characteristic U-shaped profiles (Figures 10 and 11) are classic examples of glaciated valleys. On their flanks are a series of high cwms and hanging valleys, once occupied by glaciers tributary to those in the main valleys. Cwm Idwal [645 595] is one of the largest glacial cwms and there are many other perfect examples, such as Cwm Dulyn [700 675], throughout the high peaks. The scouring effect of the debris-laden ice at the base of the ice-sheet is evident from numerous roches moutonnées with glacially striated surfaces, for example those at the head of Nant Ffrancon Pass.

Figure 11 View down Nant Ffrancon Pass from Gribin Ridge displaying well featured moraines about Llyn Idwal and the U-shaped glacial valley of Nant Ffrancon beyond. (L1890)

On the higher ground, the most distinctive depositional features of the glaciation are the moraines, for example the Darwin moraines about Llyn Idwal (Figure 12). Commonly, in such locations the moraines are not sharply defined, but are irregular hummocky spreads of boulders, gravels and clay. On the lower ground, boulder clay forms an even blanket over rockhead, as south-west of Penrhyn Castle [602 714]. The boulder clays of the two ice-sheets are quite different from each other, and there are manifold examples along the North Wales coast. That of the Irish Sea Ice is distinctively red and sandy, for much of its derived material is from the Triassic rocks which floor much of Liverpool Bay. In contrast, the local boulder clay is grey- **21**

Figure 13 Aber Falls. Face of the falls in hornfelsed mudstone bordering the Aber-Drosgl microgranodiorite intrusion. (L1944)

Figure 12 View across Llyn Idwal. On left Y Garn, Elidir Fawr in far distance, Bwlch y Cywion to Carnedd Y Filiast on right. Pitts Head Tuff outcrops through the flank and summit of Y Garn. Moraines well featured on the far side of the lake. (L1913)

brown and clayey with a preponderance of boulders of Lower Palaeozoic rocks.

On the low ground south-west of Penrhyn Castle, kames and dissected patches of outwash sands and gravels overlie the boulder clay. They were deposited by streams released from the melting ice; these were occasionally ponded against decaying ice in the lowland area.

The paths of former subglacial and marginal drainage channels can commonly still be seen, for example the network of dry channels lying contrary to the present drainage about Llanrug [540 636]. Similarly

well-developed sinuous dry channels lie on the east flank of the Conwy valley.

The results of periglacial activity, related to cycles of freezing and thawing, are particularly well displayed across the high peaks. The process continues to operate to the present day. Most of the extensive screes were initiated during the last stages of the glaciation, and they still continue to accumulate, as for example below the crags close to Aber Falls. On the flatter mountain tops, for instance across the Carneddau and between Glyder Fach and Glyder Fawr, the freeze-thaw process has created blockfields, which are made up of jumbled ice-heaved blocks. Smaller-scale features of the periglacial activity include stone polygons on flatter ground and stone stripes on slopes. Most of the slopes are smeared with head deposits, mainly gravelly clay with angular to subangular rock fragments, formed by the effects of solifluxion under periglacial conditions. Other periglacial forms such as protalus ramparts, gelifluxion lobes and altiplanation terraces are present on the high ground.

The most extensive spread of alluvium is in the floor of the Conwy valley. The alluvium probably overlies glacial outwash and boulder clay: recent geophysical work (Howells and others, 1981) has shown that the depth to bedrock varies along the longitudinal profile and is up to 130 m below the valley floor in the vicinity of Dolgarrog. River terraces are common flanking the alluvium of the major streams. Alluvial fans of varying size are also common, found where tributaries join the main valleys, such as the Conwy valley, and along Nant Ffrancon.

Peat forms an extensive cover in the high valleys to the west of the Conwy valley and between the crags on the higher ridges. Landslips are rare, although there is one on the south side of Cwm Eigiau [702 632], which is as much as 400 m across.

The Lower Palaeozoic rocks of the Bangor district were deformed and metamorphosed during the Caledonian Orogeny which, in North Wales, culminated in late Silurian to early Devonian times. Almost all the folds, together with the ubiquitous cleavage of the district, date from the Caledonian culmination. Some minor folds, however, were formed much earlier by deformation of soft sediments (Webb, 1983). Many of the major fault systems had long histories of intermittent movement extending throughout the early Palaeozoic, and radically affected the patterns of early Palaeozoic sedimentation and volcanism. Faulting continued after the Caledonian Orogeny, and folding of the Carboniferous rocks close to the Menai Straits was related to reactivation of the Dinorwic Fault system, a local manifestation of the Variscan Orogeny.

CALEDONIAN STRUCTURES

Folds   Across the entire area the rocks have been affected by folding. Folds of all scales occur, the major ones exhibiting wavelengths of several kilometres. Generally the axial-plane traces of the major folds display a north-easterly 'Caledonoid' trend, but many are sinuous with variations in trend from north-north-east to east. Such a variation is clearly displayed on the western side of the Conwy valley, where the axial-plane traces of many of the major folds affecting the Llewelyn and Snowdon Volcanic groups swing from north-east to east as the Conwy Valley Fault is approached.

Within the Cambrian and Ordovician rocks, the major folds vary in their degree of closure from open to tight. In the tight folds a common pattern is for the easterly-facing limbs to be steeply inclined or overturned and for the westerly-facing limbs to be more gently inclined. **23**

Axial planes are generally vertical or steeply inclined towards the north-west. Axial plunges vary from horizontal to steep, locally as high as 50°, and individual fold axes may display plunge culminations and depressions along their lengths with the development of subsidiary periclines, particularly in the south. In general, the fold axes plunge towards the north-east in the northern and eastern parts of the area, and display south-westerly plunges in Ordovician strata in the vicinity of the Glyder mountains and in Cambrian strata south of Deiniolen.

The variations in plunge along individual fold axes probably result from inhomogeneous strain during fold formation. Locally, as on Yr Ole Wen at the northern end of the Idwal Syncline, rapid changes in fold symmetry and axial plunge result from deformation against a relatively rigid intrusive body. The sinuosity of the axial-plane traces across the outcrop of the Llewellyn and Snowdon Volcanic groups reflects the presence of gently north-westward plunging cross-flexures.

The study of features in the rock that indicate amounts of deformation – such as reduction spots, fossils, accretionary lapilli and concretions, amongst others – shows that the amount of deformation varies markedly across the Cambrian and Ordovician outcrop. The greatest deformation is in the Cambrian slate belt of Llanberis and Bethesda (Wood, 1969; Coward and Siddans, 1979).

In contrast to the fold style in the Cambrian and Ordovician rocks, the folds in the Silurian rocks, to the east of the Conwy Valley Fault, are invariably open symmetric folds trending between east and north-east and plunging gently to the east. These trends are approximately coincident with those of folds in the adjacent Ordovician rocks to the west of the Conwy Valley Fault.

Cleavage and metamorphism A single cleavage is found throughout the Lower Palaeozoic rocks of the area, with the exception of the interior of some intrusions where cleavage is absent. The cleavage is steeply inclined and trends parallel to the axial planes of the major folds. The intensity and type of cleavage varies with the lithology: the mudstones generally display a typically slaty cleavage fabric, best developed in the Cambrian Slate Belt where deformation was particularly intense; the coarser-grained epiclastic rocks and some pyroclastic rocks and lavas generally display a more widely spaced and less well-developed cleavage.

Regional metamorphism, which accompanied the Caledonian folding, was of low grade, not exceeding the greenschist facies. Certain porphyroblastic minerals, such as chlorites in the Llanberis Slates Formation, have overgrown the cleavage and indicate that a thermal maximum postdates the strain maximum. Contact metamorphic aureoles surround some of the intrusions (Figure 13), predating the regional metamorphism.

Faults The district is strongly faulted, most faults trending either parallel to the structural grain or approximately normal to it. Among the most important fault systems are the Dinorwic and Aber Dinlle faults, traversing the north-west of the district along Caledonoid trends, and the Conwy Valley Fault system with its somewhat anomalous north-north-westerly trend. Most of the faults are steeply inclined normal faults, movement being predominantly dip-slip with no evidence of any substantial transcurrent movement.

Many of the major faults, such as the Dinorwic and Aber Dinlle faults, reflect the presence of deeper-seated basement fractures which were intermittently reactivated throughout early Palaeozoic times. The significance of faulting that was active during the deposition of Cambrian and Ordovician rocks has been mentioned in the relevant stratigraphic sections of this account; changes in the thickness of lithostratigraphic units and facies variations across some of the faults suggest that they were propagated upwards as growth-faults during sedimentation (Webb, 1983). Local unconformities at the base of the Bangor and Fachwen formations resulted from uplift and tilting along reactivated faults, and the much more extensive unconformity at the base of the Ordovician sequence also reflects differential relative uplift and tilting of fault-bounded blocks followed by erosion prior to the Arenig transgression. Penecontemporaneous faulting accompanied the Caradoc volcanic activity, and Silurian sedimentation was influenced by intermittent tectonic instability probably including movement on the Conwy Valley Fault system. During and immediately after the Caledonian folding some existing faults were reactivated and many new faults formed.

Economic geology

The local effects of mid-Carboniferous Variscan earth-movements are displayed by the early Carboniferous strata bordering the Menai Straits. Folds in the Treborth and Dinorwic formations have north-easterly-trending axes and become tighter towards the Dinorwic Fault; the main anticline within the Treborth Formation is overturned to the north-west. The rocks were buckled against the fault-bounded block of Cambrian pyroclastic and sedimentary rocks to the east, the disruption being caused by movement on the Dinorwic Fault.

The Plas Brereton Formation rests with marked angular unconformity on folded Dinantian rocks, indicating earth-movements between Dinantian and Westphalian times. Intermittent weak seismic activity associated with some of the major faults has continued into historic times.

MINING AND MINERALISATION

Iron, lead, zinc and copper minerals have been mined at a number of localities across the district. The mines were all small and were operated only sporadically, mainly during the 19th century. The factors controlling the distribution and genesis of the various ore bodies are still a matter of debate.

The deposits are of two main types: bedded sedimentary ironstones, and vein deposits of lead, zinc and copper sulphide ores occupying discordant fractures. For many years it was considered that all the vein mineralisation was epigenetic and resulted from hydrothermal activity along fractures during or after the Caledonian orogeny. More recently, evidence has shown that some mineralisation resulted from exhalations directly associated with the Ordovician volcanism. It is also possible that initially syngenetic concentrations of ore-forming elements may have been remobilised along fracture systems during a tectonic or metamorphic event. More work is needed to diagnose precisely the processes involved. Currently, much of the mineralisation is generally thought to be epigenetic, emplaced during two phases of activity, one in the early Carboniferous and one possibly in the Permian (Ineson and Mitchell, 1975).

The main area of sulphide mineralisation is the Llanrwst Mining District on the west side of the Conwy valley, mainly between the Crafnant valley in the north and the Llugwy valley in the south. The mineral potential of this area was recognised as early as 1625 (Dewey and Smith, 1922), although early attempts to exploit it were hindered by difficulties of extraction and transport. By the early 19th century access to the railway system provided a stimulus for mining and activity was greatest from about 1850 to 1914. In the following years mining declined sharply as cheaper sources were discovered elsewhere. **25**

However, the Parc Mine was worked intermittently until the later 1950s. The properties and main veins have been outlined by Howells and others (1978, 1981).

The mineralisation, mainly associated with the Snowdon Volcanic Group, is of vein type following steeply dipping normal faults which commonly show little displacement. The nature and disposition of the veins is dependent on the lithology of the country rock. In many of the most important mines dolerite occurs in the vicinity of the lodes, in places forming the wall rocks; thus the lodes post-date the intrusions. The predominant ore minerals are galena and sphalerite, although pyrite and marcasite are locally common. The main gangue minerals are quartz and calcite. Estimates drawn from the records of the quantity of ore extracted from the main mines are given by Howells and others (1981).

North of the Crafnant valley two old mine headings have been driven in the Cadnant Shales and local dolerite intrusions. The most important is the Cae Coch Mine, which is the only one in North Wales worked solely for pyrite and which originated as a syn-sedimentary deposit. Farther north in the vicinity of Henryd, lead, zinc and pyrite were extracted at the Trecastell Mine.

Copper in the form of chalcopyrite was mined from several small levels and interconnecting stopes at Clogwyn Mawr near Nant Peris [598 586] and at Derwen Deg [762 756]. The mineralised veins occupy fractures within coarse sandstones of the Bronllwyd Grit at Clogwyn Mawr and the Cadnant Shales at Derwen Deg.

Ironstone within the Nant Ffrancon Formation has been mined near Betws Garmon [544 579], Llandegai [590 696], Aber [670 724] and in the Nant Francon Pass [643 622]. The ore occurs as beds of oolitic or pisolitic chloritic mudstone up to 3.5 m thick. Associated with the ore-beds are large quantities of pyrite which crystallised during both the diagenesis and subsequent metamorphism of the sediments. The ironstones probably formed in warm shallow seas, not far offshore, at a time when the rate of subsidence was low.

AGGREGATE RESOURCES

The enormous quantities of slate waste in the tips of Dinorwic and Penrhyn quarries are a memorial to the traditional slate industry which once dominated the economy of the region. Slates are still produced at Penrhyn on a much smaller scale than in the past. The waste itself is occasionally used as low-grade fill, and studies have been made of its potential for the manufacture of lightweight expanded aggregate (Coleman and Nixon, 1974) although the results for the Cambrian slates were disappointing.

Igneous rocks abound in the district but only the microdiorite of the Penmaenmawr intrusion is now worked, from a quarry that lies just north of the district.

Sand and gravel is of limited extent in the district and is worked at Pentir, near Bangor. Sea-dredged sand is landed at Penrhyn Port.

10   References

Anderson, T., and Flett, J. S. 1903. Report on the eruptions of the Soufrière in St. Vincent in 1902 and on a visit to Montagne Pelée in Martinique, Part 1. *Philos. Trans. R. Soc., A.*, Vol. 220, 353–553.

Bassett, M. G., Owens, R. M., and Rushton, A. W. A. 1976. Lower Cambrian fossils from the Hell's Mouth Grits, St. Tudwal's Peninsula, North Wales. *J. Geol. Soc. London*, Vol. 132, 623–644.

Calver, M. A. and Smith, E. G. (1974). The Westphalian of North Wales. *In* Owen, T. R. (editor). 169–184. *The Upper Palaeozoic and post-Palaeozoic rocks of Wales* (Cardiff: University of Wales Press.)

Campbell, S. D. G. 1983. The geology of an area between Bala and Betws-y-Coed, North Wales. Unpublished PhD thesis, University of Cambridge.

Cave, R. 1965. The Nod Glas sediments of Caradoc age in North Wales. *Geol. J.*, Vol. 4, 279–298.

Chapin, C. E., and Elston, W. E. 1979. Ash-flow tuffs. *Spec. Pap. Geol. Soc. Am.*, No. 180.

Clarke, J. W., and Hughes, T. McK. 1980. Life and letters of the Rev. Adam Sedgwick. (Cambridge.)

Coleman, E. H., and Nixon, P. J. *1974. A survey of possible* sources in Wales of raw materials for the manufacture of a lightweight expanded slate aggregate. *Current Pap. Building Res. Establishment*, No. 78/74, 1–15.

Coward, M. P., and Siddans, A. W. B. 1979. The tectonic evolution of the Welsh Caledonides. *In* **Harris, A. L., Holland, C. H., and Leake, R. E.** (Editors), *The Caledonides of the British Isles—reviewed*, 187–198. *Spec. Pub. Geol. Soc. London*, No. 8.

Crimes, T. P. 1970. Trilobite tracks and other trace fossils from the Upper Cambrian of North Wales. *Geol. J.*, Vol. 7, 47–68.

Davies, D. A. B. 1936. Ordovician rocks of the Trefriw district (North Wales). *Q. J. Geol. Soc. London*, Vol. 92, 62–90.

Dean, W. T. 1965. A shelly fauna from the Snowdon Volcanic Series at Twll du, Caernarvonshire. *Geol. J.*, Vol. 4, 301–314.

Dewey, H., and Smith, B. 1922. Lead and zinc ores in the pre Carboniferous rocks of West Shropshire and North Wales, part 1, North Wales. *Spec. Rep. Miner Resour., Mem. Geol. Surv. GB*, Vol. 23.

Elles, G. L. 1909. The relationship of the Ordovician and Silurian rocks of Conwy (North Wales). *Q. J. Geol. Soc. London*, Vol. 65, 169–194.

Francis, E. H., and Howells, M. F. 1973. Transgressive welded ash-flow tuffs among the Ordovician sediments of N.E. Snowdonia, N. Wales. *J. Geol. Soc. London*, Vol. 129, 621–641.

Greenly, E. 1919. Geology of Anglesey. *Mem. Geol. Surv. GB.*

Greenly, E. 1928. The Lower Carboniferous rocks of the Menaian region of Carnarvonshire: their petrology, succession and physiography. *Q. J. Geol. Soc. London*, Vol. 84, 382–439.

Greenly, E. 1938. The red measures of the Menaian region of Caernarvonshire. *Q. J. Geol. Soc. London*, Vol. 94, 331–345.

Greenly, E. 1944. The Ordovician rocks of Arvon. *Q. J. Geol. Soc. London*, Vol. 100, 75–83.

Greenly, E. 1945. The Arvonian rocks of Arvon. *Q. J. Geol. Soc. London*, Vol. 100, 269–284.

Greenly, E. 1946. The geology of the city of Bangor. *Proc. Liverpool Geol. Soc.*, Vol. 19, 105–112.

George, T. N. *1974. Lower Carboniferous rocks in Wales. In* Owen, T. R. (Editor), *The Upper Palaeozoic and post-Palaeozoic rocks of Wales*, 85–116 (Cardiff: University of Wales Press.)

George, T. N., Johnson, G. A. L., Mitchell, M., Prentice, J. E., Ramsbottom, W. H. C., Sevastopulo, G. D., and

Wilson, R. B. 1976. A correlation of Dinantian rocks in the British Isles. *Spec. Rep. Geol. Soc. London*, No. 7.

Harker, A. 1889. *The Bala Volcanic Series of Caernarvonshire.* (Cambridge.)

Harland, W. D., and Gayer, R. A. 1972. The Arctic Caledonides and earlier oceans. *Geol. Mag.*, Vol. 109, 289–314.

Hibbert, F. A., and Lacey, W. S. 1969. Miospores from the Lower Carboniferous Basement Beds in the Menai Straits region of Caernarvonshire, North Wales. *Palaeontology*, Vol. 12, 420–440.

Howell, B. F. and Stubblefield, C. J. A revision of the fauna of the North Welsh *Conocoryphe viola* Beds, implying a Lower Cambrian age. *Geol. Mag.*, Vol. 87, 1–16.

Howells, M. F., Leveridge, B. E., and Evans, C. D. R. *1971.* The Lower Crafnant Volcanic Group, eastern Snowdonia. *Proc. Geol. Soc. London*, No. 1664, 284–285.

Howells, M. F., Leveridge, B. E. and Evans, C. D. R. 1973. Ordovician ash-flow tuffs in eastern Snowdonia. *Rep. Inst. Geol. Sci.*, No. 73/3.

Howells, M. F. 1977. The varying pattern of volcanicity and sedimentation in the Bedded Pyroclastic Formation and Middle Crafnant Volcanic Formation in the Ordovician of central and eastern Snowdonia. *J. Geol. Soc. London*, Vol. 133, abstract.

Howells, M. F., Francis, E. H., Leveridge, B. E. and Evans, C. D. R. 1978. *Capel Curig and Betws-y-Coed: Description of 1:25 000 sheet SH 75.* Classical areas of British geology, Institute of Geological Sciences. (London: HMSO.)

Howells, M. F., and Leveridge, B. E. 1980. The Capel Curig Volcanic Formation. *Rep. Inst. Geol. Sci.*, No. 80/6.

Howells, M. F., Leveridge, B. E., Evans, C. D. R., and Nutt, M. J. C. 1981. *Dolgarrog: Description of 1:25 000 geological sheet SH 76.* Classical areas of British geology, Institute of Geological Sciences. (London: HMSO.)

Howells, M. F., Leveridge, B. E., Reedman, A. J., and Addison, R. 1983. The lithostratigraphical subdivision of the *Ordovician underlying the Snowdon and Crafnant Volcanic* Groups, North Wales. *Rep. Inst. Geol. Sci.*, No. 83/1, 11–15.

Howells, M. F., Leveridge, B. E., Evans, C. D. R. and Addison, R. *In press. The passes of Nant Ffrancon and Llanberis: Description of 1:25 000 sheet SH 65N/66S.* Classical areas of British geology, Institute of Geological Sciences (London: HMSO.)

Ineson, P. R., and Mitchell, J. G. 1975. K-Ar isotopic age determinations from some Welsh mineral localities. *Trans. Inst. Min. Metall. London, B: Appl. Earth Sci.*, Vol. 84, B7–16.

Jackson, D. E. 1961. Stratigraphy of the Skiddaw Group between Buttermere and Mungrisdale, Cumberland. *Geol. Mag.*, Vol. 98, 548–550.

Jones, O. T. 1938. On the evolution of a geosyncline (Anniversary address). *Q. J. Geol. Soc. London*, Vol. 94, lx–cx.

Lacroix, A. 1903. L'éruption de la Montagne Pelée en janvier 1903. *C. R. Acad. Sci. (Paris)*, Vol. 136, 442–445.

Lacroix, A. 1904. La Montagne Pelée et ses éruptions. (Paris: Masson et cie.)

Marshall, P. 1935. Acid rocks of Taupo Rotorua volcanic district. *Trans. R. Soc. N.Z.*, Vol. 64, 323–366.

Oliver, R. L. *1954. Welded tuffs in the Borrowdale Volcanic* Series, English Lake District, with a note on similar rocks in Wales. *Geol. Mag.*, Vol. 91, 473–483.

Price, D. 1977. Species of *Tretaspis* (Trilobita) from the Ashgill Series in Wales. *Palaeontology*, Vol. 20, 763–792.

Ramsay, A. C. 1866. The geology of North Wales. *Mem. Geol. Surv. GB*, Vol. 3.

Ramsay, A. C. 1881. The geology of North Wales (2nd edition). *Mem. Geol. Surv. GB*, Vol. 3.

Rast, N., Beavon, R. V., and Fitch, F. J. 1958. Subaerial volcanicity in Snowdonia. *Nature, London*, Vol. 181, 508.

Reedman, A. J., Leveridge, B. E., and Evans, R. B. 1984. The early Cambrian Arfon Basin of N.W. Wales. *Proc. Geol. Ass.*, Vol. 95, 313–321.

Reedman, A. J., Webb, B. C., Leveridge, B. E., and Howells, M. F. 1983. The Cambrian–Ordovician boundary between Aber and Betws Garmon, Gwynedd, North Wales. *Rep. Inst. Geol. Sci.*, No. 83/1, 7–10.

Roberts, B. 1967. Succession and structure in the Llwyd Mawr Syncline, Caernarvonshire, North Wales. *Geol. J.*, Vol. 5, 369–390.

Ross, C. S., and Smith, R. L. 1961. Ash-flow tuffs: their origin, geological relations and identification. *Prof. Pap. US Geol. Surv.*, No. 366.

Sedgwick, A. 1845. On the older Palaeozoic (protozoic) rocks of North Wales. *Q. J. Geol. Soc. London*, Vol. 1, 5–22.

Sharpe, D. 1846. Contributions to the geology of North Wales. *Q. J. Geol. Soc. London*, Vol. 2, 283–316.

Smith, R. L. 1960a. Ash-flows. *Bull. Geol. Soc. Am.*, Vol. 71, 795–842.

Smith, R. L. 1960b. Zones and zonal variations in welded ash-flows. *Prof. Pap. US Geol. Surv.*, No. 354-f.

Stevenson, I. P. 1971. The Ordovician rocks of the country between Dwygyfylchi and Dolgarrog, Caernarvonshire. *Proc. Yorkshire Geol. Soc.*, Vol. 38, 517–548.

Warren, P. T., Price, D., Nutt, M. J. C., and Smith, E. G. 1984. Geology of the country around Rhyl and Denbigh. *Mem. Geol. Surv. GB*, Sheets 95 and 107.

Webb, B. C. 1983. Early Caledonian structures in the Cambrian Slate Belt, Gwynedd, North Wales. *Rep. Inst. Geol. Sci.*, No. 83/1, 1–6.

Whittow, J. B., and Ball, D. F. 1970. North-west Wales. *In* Lewis, C. A. (editor), *The glaciation of Wales and adjoining regions*, 21–28 (London: Longmans.)

Williams, D. 1930. The geology of the country between Nant Peris and Nant Ffrancon (Snowdonia). *Q. J. Geol. Soc. London*, Vol. 86, 191–233.

Williams, H. 1922. The igneous rocks of the Capel Curig District (North Wales). *Proc. Liverpool Geol. Soc.*, Vol. 13, 166–202.

Williams, H. 1927. The geology of Snowdon (North Wales). *Q. J. Geol. Soc. London*, Vol. 83, 346–431.

Williams, H., and Bulman, O. M. B. 1931. The geology of the Dolwyddelan Syncline (North Wales). *Q. J. Geol. Soc. London*, Vol. 87, 425–458.

Wilson, J. T. 1966. Did the Atlantic close and then re-open? *Nature, London*, Vol. 211, 676–681.

Wood, D. S. 1969. The base and correlation of the Cambrian rocks of North Wales. *In* Wood, A. (editor), *The Precambrian and Lower Palaeozoic rocks of Wales*, 47–66. (Cardiff: University of Wales Press.)

11 Glossary of geological terms

Acid   Relating to igneous rocks containing more than 66% of silica.

Accretionary lapilli   Small pea sized aggregations of volcanic ash that formed about nuclei, such as drops of moisture, during fall through the air following eruption from a volcano.

Agglomerate   A volcanic rock formed of pyroclastic blocks or fragments of generally more than 50 mm diameter and which were ejected in a plastic state.

Air-fall tuff   A tuff formed by the showerlike gravitational settling of pyroclastic debris from an eruption cloud.

Alluvial fan   A gently sloping apron of loose rock material, shaped in plan like an open fan, and deposited by a stream at a point where the gradient of the stream decreases abruptly. An alluvial cone is similar in form but slopes more steeply.

Altiplanation terrace   A broad terrace formed under periglacial conditions and often comprising an accumulation of gelifluxed superficial deposits on a very low angle slope.

Amygdale   A gas cavity in an igneous rock filled with secondary minerals.

Anticline   A fold, convex upwards, so that the stratigraphically older rocks are contained in the core.

Argillaceous   Containing clay-sized particles of clay minerals.

Ash-flow   A turbulent mixture of pyroclastic debris and hot gas which flows in directions determined by the originating explosive volcanic eruption and by gravity.

Ash-flow tuff   A tuff composed of pyroclastic debris deposited from an ash-flow.

Autobreccia   A breccia formed by a process which is contemporaneous with the formation of the rock unit from which the fragments are derived: particularly in a flowing lava or intrusion where the consolidated outer crust fractures and the fragments are incorporated into the still-fluid portion.

Axial plane   A plane that connects the hinges of all the individual folded beds within the fold. In a syncline it connects the troughs of each folded layer and in an anticline it connects the crests.

Axial plunge   The inclination of a fold axis.

Basalt   A fine-grained basic lava or minor intrusion composed mainly of calcic plagioclase and pyroxene, with or ·ithout olivine.

Basic   Pertaining to igneous rocks containing less than 52% of silica.

Bioclastic   Consisting of complete or fragmental organic material, usually shells.

Biostratigraphy   The separation and differentiation of rock units on the basis of the fossils they contain.

Bioturbation   The disturbance or churning of sediment by organisms.

Boulder clay (till)   An unconsolidated and unstratified deposit of clay with boulders deposited beneath an ice sheet or glacier.

Breccia   A coarse-grained clastic rock composed of angular rock fragments set in finer grained matrix.

Caldera   A large basin-shaped volcanic depression, more or less circular in form.

Caledonian orogeny   Major earth movements of Lower Palaeozoic age which reached their culmination at the end of the Silurian.

Caledonides   The folded mountain chain which resulted from the Caledonian orogeny; the Caledonian orogenic belt.

Caliche A concretionary development of calcium carbonate within the upper part of a soil profile.

Clast An individual fragment of rock of mineral produced by the erosion or mechanical disintegration of a larger rock mass.

Clastic rock A rock composed of clasts.

Cleavage Cleavage (in a rock) is a parallel planar fabric produced by deformation of the rock resulting in a tendency for the rock to split along closely spaced parallel planes.

Columnar joints Fractures which form by contraction during cooling of igneous rocks and disposed such that sets of the factures form parallel prismatic columns within the rock. Most commonly found in lava flows and certain minor intrusions.

Convolute lamination Contorted bedding laminae which are confined to a single well defined layer within a bedded sequence and are both overlain and underlain by parallel undisturbed layers.

Cross-bedding An internal arrangement of the layers in a stratified sediment characterised by parallel sloping minor layers deposited at an angle to the principal stratification.

Diagenesis The chemical, physical and biological modifications undergone by a sediment after deposition, during and after transformation to a rock but excluding subsequent metamorphism and superficial weathering.

Distal Remote from the source area.

Dolerite A medium-grained igneous rock generally forming minor intrusions and consisting mainly of calcic plagioclase and pyroxene, commonly with an ophitic texture.

Dyke A tabular igneous intrusion that cuts across the bedding or primary planar structures of the enclosing rock.

Epiclastic rocks Sedimentary rocks formed of fragments derived by the weathering and erosion of older rocks.

Epigenetic ore Ore formed later than the rocks in which it occurs.

Eruption column An approximately cylindrical column of gas and pyroclastic debris emitted from the vent of a volcano during an explosive eruption.

Extrusive igneous rocks Volcanic rocks formed by the eruption of material on to the surface of the Earth; includes lavas and pyroclastic rocks.

Facies (sedimentary) The total lithological and palaeontological character of a rock from which its origin and environment of formation may be deduced.

Flow bands Alternating layers of contrasting texture and/or composition in an igneous rock, formed as a result of flow in a magma.

Fluvial sediment A sediment laid down by a stream or river.

Gangue The uneconomic minerals in an orebody.

Gelifluxion The progressive flow of soil and superficial material under periglacial freeze-thaw conditions.

Glacial striation A groove or scratch on a rock surface caused by rock fragments embedded in the base of a moving glacier being dragged across the surface.

Graded bedding Internal structure of a clastic sediment whereby the maximum grain size progressively decreases from the base to the top of the bed.

Growth fault A fault in sediments or tuffs that forms contemporaneously and continuously with deposition so that the throw increases with depth.

Hornfels An equigranular, unfoliated, fine grained rock formed by metamorphic crystallisation of wallrocks during the emplacement of an igneous intrusion.

Hyaloclastite A deposit composed of comminuted basaltic glass formed by the fragmentation of the glassy skins of basaltic pillows or by the violent eruption of basalt under the sea.

Hydrothermal Pertaining to heated water, for example a mineral deposit precipitated from a hot aqueous solution.

Intermediate Relating to igneous rocks transitional between acid and basic.

Intrusive igneous rock An igneous rock formed from magma injected into the Earth's crust.

Kame A mound of poorly sorted sand and gravel deposited from a sub-glacial stream near the margin of a melting glacier.

Lithic Pertaining to rock.

Lithification The process whereby unconsolidated material becomes converted to rock; the consolidation and induration of sediment or pyroclastic volcanic debris.

Metamorphism The recrystallisation and mineralogical adjustment of a rock in response to changes in temperature and pressure during its history other than superficial changes in the zone of weathering.

Moraine A mound or ridge of unsorted and unstratified glacial debris deposited by the direct action of glacier ice.

Mudflow breccia A rock consisting of angular clasts (many of mudstone), in a mudstone matrix and formed by the downslope collapse and mass flow of pre-existing, muddy sediment.

Pericline A fold in which the dip of the folded beds has a central orientation; in a dome the beds dip away from the centre, in a basin they dip towards the centre.

Periglacial Pertaining to processes and conditions at the periphery of glaciated areas where frost action is a significant factor.

Phenocrysts Relatively large conspicuous crystals within a finer groundmass in magmatic igneous rocks.

Pillow breccia A rock composed of fragments of broken pillow lava.

Pillow lava A rock mass composed of closely packed discontinuous spheroidal masses of lava. Pillows most commonly form in basaltic lava extruded into a subaqueous environment.

Pisolitic Pertaining to a rock containing pisoliths: spherical or ellipsoidal accretionary bodies of sedimentary origin 2–10 mm in diameter.

Plate tectonics A global tectonic model based on the proposal that the outer part of the Earth comprises a number of internally rigid but relatively thin plates, about 100–150 km thick, which are continually in motion with respect to each other.

Porphyroblast A relatively large and conspicuous crystal in a metamorphic rock.

Protalus rampart An arcuate ridge of loose boulders formed at the downslope edge of a snowbank.

Proximal Close to the source area.

Pumice A highly vesiculated rock composed of frothy glassy lava light enough to float on water; recrystallised fragments of pumice commonly occur in the tuffs of North Wales.

Pyroclastic breccia A volcanic rock consisting of large angular fragments of material which have been fragmented, produced and erupted in a solid state by explosive volcanic activity.

Pyroclastic rock A clastic volcanic rock composed of material fragmented and erupted by explosive volcanic activity.

Reduction spots Light-coloured spheroidal patches within red and purple siltstones and mudstones produced by a local change in the content or oxidation state of iron within the spot.

Reworking In this account 'reworking' refers to the removal and redeposition by water of recently deposited tuff or sediment.

Rhyolite An extrusive igneous rock of acid composition, commonly porphyritic and flow banded.

Seat earth A bed underlying a coal seam representing an old soil which supported the vegetation from which the coal subsequently formed.

Sill A tubular igneous intrusion that parallels the bedding or primary planar structures of the enclosing rock.

Shard A small fragment of glass having cuspate margins, frequently spindle shaped, and commonly found in pyroclastic rocks.

Slumped beds Beds distorted by subaqueous sliding or lateral movement of unconsolidated sediment.

Stone polygons A polygonal arrangement of loose rock fragments in near-surface superficial material formed by freeze-thaw action.

Syncline A fold, concave upwards, such that the stratigraphically younger strata are contained in the core.

Syngenetic ore Ore formed at the same time as the enclosing rocks.

Tectonics A branch of geology dealing with the regional aspects of the structural and deformational features of the earth's crust including their mutual relations, origin and historical evolution.

Trace fossil A fossilised track, burrow, tube or boring resulting from the activity of animal, for example a mark made by an invertebrate creeping across the surface of sediment at the time of its accumulation.

Tuff A lithified deposit of volcanic ash.

Tuffite A rock consisting of a mixture of pyroclastic (>25%) and epiclastic (>25%) fragments.

Turbidite A sediment deposited from a turbidity flow.

Turbidity flow A dense subaqueous flow of water and suspended sediment which moves downslope by gravity.

Unconformity A substantial gap in the geologic record where a rock unit is overlain by another that is not next in stratigraphic succession. Commonly the younger strata lie with angular discordance on the older strata implying a period of uplift and erosion between the periods of deposition of the two sets of strata.

Vesicle A small bubble-like cavity in a lava, formed by included gas.

Volcanogenic sediment A sediment whose origin is in some way associated with volcanic activity.

Welding foliation A parallel planar fabric formed by the flattening of hot plastic glass and pumice fragments during welding in a tuff.

Welded tuff A tuff in which the hot, plastic pyroclastic fragments have been agglutinated under the influence of retained heat and the weight of overlying material.

Maps at 1:10 000 scale   Complete cover for the district. See index on 1:50 000 map. Manuscript copies on plastic available for consultation. Surveyed 1967–80.

Maps at 1:25 000 scale
SH 55/56   In press (1985)
SH 64/65   In press (1985)
SH 65/66   In press (1985)
SH 66/67   In press (1985)
SH 76   Published with accompanying handbook
SH 75   Published with accompanying handbook
SH 77/78   In press (1985)

Photographs   Albums of coloured/black and white prints are available for consultation. They illustrate the full range of the geology of the district. All these photographs are available also as 35 mm colour slides.

Rock samples   A full range of thin sections has been cut and used in describing the district. They are available for consultation on request.

Boreholes   There are no deep boreholes in the district but shallow drilling results are available for consultation; they mostly relate to the coastal area.

Consultation   In the first instance enquiries about the district should be directed to the Regional Office for Wales, Bryn Eithyn Hall, Llanfarian, Aberystwyth, Dyfed SY23 4BY (Aberystwyth [0970] 611038). Most material may be inspected, by appointment only, at the Aberystwyth office, but some is also available at the headquarters of BGS, Keyworth, Nottingham NG12 5GG (Plumtree [060 77] 6111).

1   Please obey the Country Code. Remember to shut gates and leave no litter.

2   Always seek permission before entering private land. Enclose a stamped addressed envelope when asking to visit sites.

3   Don't litter fields or roads with rock fragments. If you have a geological hammer, use it sparingly; indiscriminate hammering damages outcrops for those who come after.

4   Keep collecting to an absolute minimum. Better still, take your specimens away as photographs. If they are needed for bona-fide study, collect only from fallen blocks.

5   Beware of dangerous cliffs and rock faces. Wear safety helmets where advisable.

6   Take local advice on tide conditions.

7   Before working in mountains ensure that you are properly equipped, and inform someone of your intended route and estimated time of return.

Dd 737398   C20

Printed in England for HMSO by Commercial Colour Press, London E7.